A Gift of Compassion...

To: _____

From: _____

❧·❧

Dedication

I dedicate this book to my husband Craig for his willingness to grow in compassion with me. There is nothing more important in this life than those who are closest to us. Their love, happiness and time together is what makes a difference.

I'd like to dedicate this book to our entire loving family. I want to give my heartfelt recognition to our joined family, Craig's daughters and their husbands, Marisa and Dustin and Alexa and Thomas, and all the joy they continuously bring us.

I also dedicate this book to my son, Brynie James for giving me a reason to keep going forward when times past were challenging and jam-packed full of opportunity to learn compassion for myself and then give it to others.

Mary Robinson Reynolds

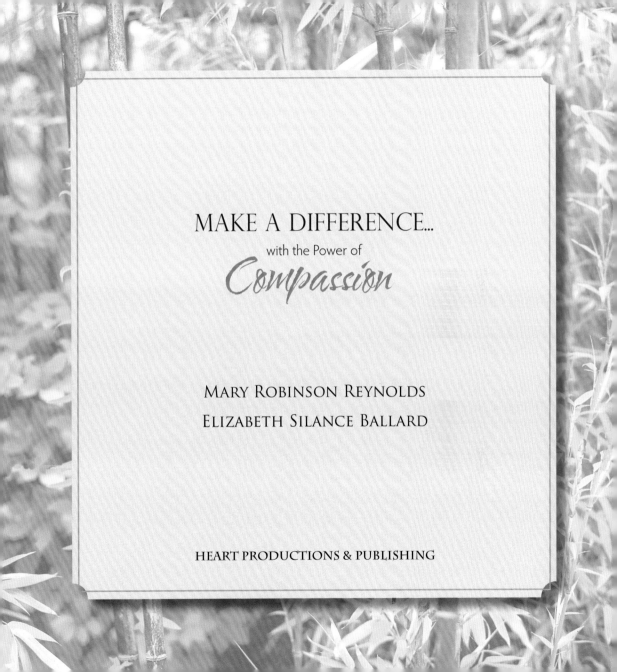

MAKE A DIFFERENCE...

with the Power of

Compassion

MARY ROBINSON REYNOLDS

ELIZABETH SILANCE BALLARD

HEART PRODUCTIONS & PUBLISHING

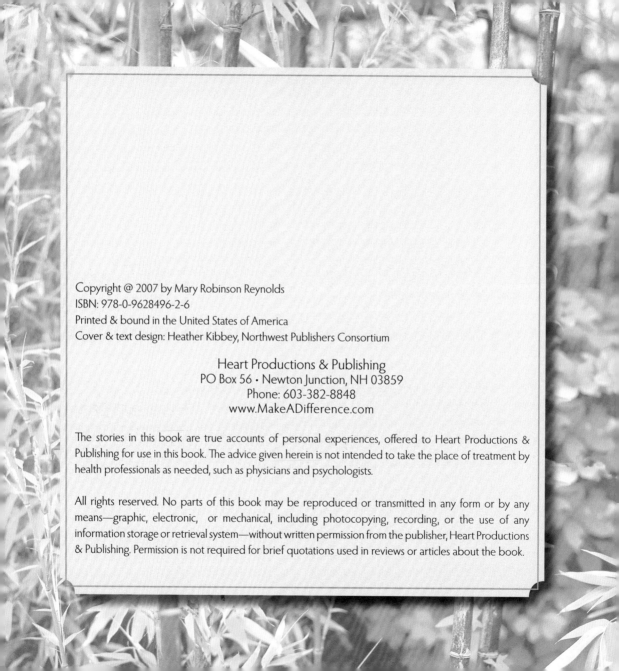

Heart Productions & Publishing
PO Box 56 · Newton Junction, NH 03859
Phone: 603-382-8848
www.MakeADifference.com

The stories in this book are true accounts of personal experiences, offered to Heart Productions & Publishing for use in this book. The advice given herein is not intended to take the place of treatment by health professionals as needed, such as physicians and psychologists.

Table of Contents

Straight to The Heart

*C*ompassion is the universal language of humanity. And that's the reason the poignant story of Teddy Stallard has a magnetic quality—its message is understood the world over.

I felt compelled to create the flash movie from a story written by Elizabeth Silance Ballard because it is such a positive reminder of how we can completely turn around a life with the power of compassion. Originally published in a significantly different form in a 1974 issue of Home Life magazine as *Three Letters from Teddy*, this fictional tale has been passed from person to person as a "true" account for over three decades.

This is a story that bypasses the head and goes straight to the heart. Teddy Stallard's story illustrates what happens when a person stops judging and starts connecting. Compassion creates a real possibility for what can happen in all human interactions, when a simple willingness to understand brings about a life-altering "shift in perception."

The Creation of a Flash Movie

My entrepreneurial trek, which has included work with adults and children in educational, corporate and personal settings, began nearly twenty years ago when I started to realize I knew something about at-risk youth that a large percentage of the educators I worked with had not yet discovered.

My special gift was that I knew, intuitively, how to heal behaviorally challenging children. My ability to create for them a sense of community and "belonging" helped them achieve measurably high levels of success, no matter how overcrowded my classrooms were.

I realized early into my teaching career that I had mentally done away with the "bell curve" and the "labels" put on behaviorally and academically challenged children by other well-meaning teachers before me. When, as a sixth-grade teacher, I collected data from previous years of Stanford Achievement Test results, I found that the children arriving in my classroom each year were, on average, a year or two behind their expected grade level. With my determination and guidance, through the elimination of labels and engaging instruction, they not only gained back what they had previously lost, but they achieved an additional two to three years of academic growth on their Stanford Achievement Test results.

In 1988, when I understood the effectiveness of my techniques, I began writing continuing educational programs to assist educators in learning how to heal all of the students in their classrooms who were living unhappy lives and not succeeding academically or otherwise. The results of these programs were even more amazing than I could have predicted—teachers were now armed with the tools they needed to deal compassionately and effectively with difficult children.

Then life happened! Legislation was passed in Oregon to cut all funding for school programs such as mine. As a single parent, I needed to create income immediately.

I found myself redirected—led—into the corporate arena, where I quickly realized that we are all just little kids in big bodies! The principles and strategies I had been teaching educators, about breaking cycles of failure, worked in very diverse business environments as well.

We're all just little kids in big bodies.

I realized that in working with adults in corporations, and teaching them how to heal and deal powerfully with their own lives in and away from the workplace, I would, in effect, be helping children after all. When parents learned how to heal themselves through the principles I taught them, their children would be well. So I found great peace with the fact that, although I was no longer working directly in the educational arena, my teaching was having a positive effect on adults and their children alike.

Now, nearly two decades later, I have spoken in every major city in the United States about the power of labeling and attitudes in communication. I've spoken to tens of thousands of people, written five books, and started writing motivational poetry again for the first time since I was 18. My poems have become flash online movies and are available for anyone to watch at no charge and to pass along to others who would appreciate them. You'll find them at www.MakeADifference.com.

I also knew that I had come full circle.

And this brings us to 2006, when I was sent a musical rendition of the Teddy Stallard story. I knew in a heartbeat that it needed to be a flash movie. I also knew that I had come full circle.

And now I'd like to share with you the story that has touched the hearts of so many who've heard it, Elizabeth Silance Ballard's heartwarming tale of the power of compassion to change a life:

Three Letters from Teddy

from the

MAKE A DIFFERENCE MOVIE

On the following pages you'll be entranced as the story unfolds, through images from the *Make A Difference Movie*. And following this, the author, Elizabeth Silance Ballard, will continue to weave the magic of her storytelling as she relates the true–life basis for this wonderful work.

12

*A*s she stood in front
of her 5th grade class
on the first day of school,
she told the children

an untruth.

Like most teachers,
she looked at her students
and said that she loved them
all the same.

*H*owever, that was

impossible,

because there in the front row,

slumped in his seat,

was a little boy named

Teddy Stallard.

$\mathcal{M}$iss Thompson had watched Teddy
the year before and noticed that
he didn't play well with other children,
that his clothes were messy,
and that he constantly

needed a bath.

17

*A*nd, Teddy could be *unpleasant.*

It got to the point where Miss Thompson
would actually take delight
in marking his papers with a broad red pen...

making bold X's

and then putting a big

'F'

at the top of his papers.

At the school where Miss Thompson taught,
she was required to review
each child's past records,
and she put Teddy's off until the last.

However, when she reviewed his file,

she was in for a surprise.

Teddy's first grade teacher wrote:
"Teddy is a bright child with a ready laugh.
He does his work neatly and
has good manners.
He is such a joy to be around."

*H*is second grade teacher wrote:
"Teddy is an excellent student,
well liked by his classmates,

but he is troubled

because his mother has a
terminal illness,
and life at home must be a struggle."

*H*is third grade teacher wrote:

"His mother's death has been hard on him.
He tries to do his best,
but his father doesn't

show much interest,

and his home life will soon affect him
if some steps aren't taken."

*T*eddy's fourth grade teacher wrote:

"Teddy is

withdrawn

and doesn't show much interest in school.
He doesn't have many friends
and he sometimes
sleeps in class."

By now, Miss Thompson
realized the problem, and she was
ashamed of herself.

She felt even worse
when her students brought her
Christmas presents,
wrapped in beautiful ribbons and bright paper,

except for Teddy's.

31

*H*is present was clumsily wrapped

in the heavy brown paper

that he got from a grocery bag.

Miss Thompson took pains to open

it in the middle of the other presents.

Some of the students started to laugh

when she found a rhinestone bracelet

with some of the stones

missing

and a bottle that was

one-quarter full

of perfume.

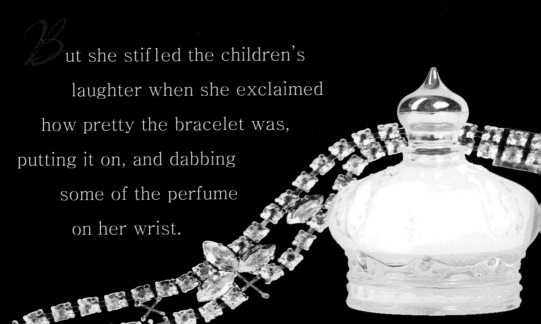

*B*ut she stifled the children's

laughter when she exclaimed

how pretty the bracelet was,

putting it on, and dabbing

some of the perfume

on her wrist.

Teddy Stallard

stayed after school that day

just long enough to say,

"Miss Thompson, today you smell

just like my Mom used to."

After the children left she cried
for at least an hour.

On that very day, she quit teaching
reading, writing and arithmetic.

*Instead, she began
to teach children.*

$\mathcal{M}$iss Thompson paid particular

attention to Teddy.

As she worked with him,

his mind began to come alive.

The more she encouraged him,

the faster he responded.

By the end of the year, Teddy had become

one of the smartest children in the class,

and despite her lie that she would

love all the children the same,

Teddy became one of her

"*teacher's pets.*"

A year later,
she found a note under
her door from Teddy,
telling her that she was

the best teacher

he'd ever had
in his whole life!

ear Miss Thompson,
You are the best
teacher I've ever
had in my whole life!

Teddy

Six years went by before she got
another note from Teddy.

He then wrote that he had finished high school
third in his class, and she was still

the best teacher

he ever had in his whole life.

*F*our years after that,

      she got another letter,

saying that while things had been

tough at times, he'd stayed in school.

He'd stuck with it, and would soon

graduate from college with the

highest of honors.

Again he assured Miss Thompson

      that she was still the best and

favorite teacher he'd ever had.

43

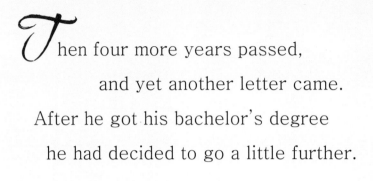

Then four more years passed,
and yet another letter came.
After he got his bachelor's degree
he had decided to go a little further.

She was still the best and
favorite teacher he'd ever had.
But now his name was
a little longer...
the letter was signed

Theodore F. Stallard, M.D.

44

The story does not end here.

There was yet another letter that spring.

Teddy said he'd met this girl...

and was going to be

married.

He explained that his father had died
a couple of years ago, and he was wondering
if Miss Thompson might agree
to sit at the wedding in the place that was usually
reserved for the mother of the groom.

Of course, Miss Thompson did.
And guess what?
She wore that bracelet,
the one with several rhinestones missing.
Moreover, she made sure she was wearing
the perfume that Teddy remembered
his mother wearing
on their last Christmas together.

50

They hugged each other, and
Dr. Stallard whispered in Miss Thompson's ear:

"Thank you for believing in me.

Thank you so much
for making me feel important and
showing me that I could make a difference."

$\mathcal{M}$iss Thompson, with tears in her eyes,

whispered back.

She said, "Teddy you have it all wrong.

You were the one who taught me that I could

make a difference.

I didn't know how to teach until I met you!"

53

You can never tell...

what type of impact

you may have

on another's life

by your actions...

or lack of action.

Please consider this fact

in your venture through life,

and just try to...

make a difference

in someone else's life today.

But that's not all ...

From the moment my "Tech Genius" husband, Craig, and I began the creation of the movie, I started searching the Internet for Elizabeth Silance Ballard, author of the Teddy Stallard story. Early in 2007, I found her. She had just released her new book, *Three Letters from Teddy and Other Stories*, which we are now honored to carry in our website Gift Store.

So now I am thrilled to be able to introduce to you the author of the Teddy Stallard Story, as she describes the origin of this endearing work...

From Elizabeth to You ...

The story behind *"Three Letters from Teddy"*

"My friend was a 'sub' for a teacher on maternity leave many years ago. She happened to be there at Christmas and was touched at a gift a child had given to her at the class party: a rhinestone bracelet with stones missing and a small bottle of perfume, half empty.

"As she was telling this, I zipped back in memory to when I was in the fourth grade and I wanted to give the teacher a gift. My parents told me 'We can't afford to give presents to everybody. You drew a name and that's the present we will have to buy. The teacher doesn't expect presents from everybody.'

"Well, I loved Mrs. Clinard and I wanted to give her something. I cried and cried and then my grandmother had an idea. We got a shoe box, went out into her back yard and picked up pecans. I was a little ashamed of this 'gift' but Grandmama assured me anyone would be glad to get such nice pecans.

"Sure enough, when my gift was opened, all the kids snickered and laughed. One girl even said, 'What kind of present is that? It doesn't even have a bow!'

"Mrs. Clinard just squealed and smiled and said, 'Oh, thank you, Elizabeth. I've got lots of company coming and I needed some nuts for my fruitcake! You were so sweet to think of this!' And she hugged me.

"Well, she validated not just my gift but somehow she also validated me. I've never forgotten Mrs. Clinard, who taught 4th grade at Walter M. Thompson Elementary School in Jacksonville, NC during the school year of 1952–1953. I can't remember her first name and I can't find my report cards but I would love for Mrs Clinard to know that 'Miss Thompson' was based on her and how much she had meant to a little girl who felt pretty worthless at the time.

"Mrs. Clinard's compassionate response, coupled with my friend's story formed the basis for the Teddy Stallard story. Teddy's last name came from combining the surname of my grandmother (Stanley) who urged me to bring pecans to my teacher with my then surname (Ballard) to form Stallard."

Make A Difference with...
The Power of Compassion

This is a story about more than kindness; it's about the essence and the power that compassion offers all humanity.

Many of us cry every time we watch this movie. Perhaps it's because we wish we'd had someone in our lives who had shown us that compassion. Or maybe it reminds us of all the special people who have made a difference in our lives and we cry with gratitude.

After the movie's debut, I received hundreds of inspiring stories from all over the world—personal narratives that describe how this story of Teddy has ignited compassion and understanding. For this beautiful book, I selected stories that captured the essence of "making a difference...with compassion" in seven different ways.

Compassion

Igniting Compassion

The choice was difficult. For example, a 6 ft. 2 in., 250–pound construction worker by the name of Walter Wood wrote to tell me that he felt this short, but profound, film actually brought tears to his eyes. He said it made him realize that he must be more mindful when he's training his apprentices.

Edmond Nickson wrote: "The Teddy Stallard story may have been written as fiction, but not for me. As I watched the movie, I was moved to tears. It brought back the pain of my mother's sudden death at age 39 from sleeping sickness, likely brought on by a mosquito bite. I was 12. I found her in a coma and was unable to wake her. Two very long weeks later, she was gone.

"As my father woke me and my sister with the news, I thought, 'Who's going to love me now?' Thank you for the beautiful Teddy Stallard story that you turned into a flash movie. It touched an old wound that once again reopened, allowing me to heal at a deeper level. Blessings to you."

Rowena Castro sent this note: "I would like to express my sincere congratulations for a wonderful movie you so generously shared with your readers. As a student affairs practitioner, I really appreciate the value of teaching, not only academically but more so on the total development of an individual—psychologically, spiritually and emotionally. I shared the movie with my co-workers and we all shared the tears, as we felt in our hearts the job we are doing in molding hearts and minds of young people."

Even though this story is fiction, its message is universal. It's unifying because it transcends the need to use force to counter unacceptable behavior that arises in disturbing circumstances and situations where an individual feels beyond his or her own control.

We've all thought from time to time, "I just wish so and so would learn to be caring—or 'generous' or 'accommodating'—to others, and be more compassionate like Miss Thompson."

Its message is universal.

As with Teddy, we somehow expect people in pain to figure it out and "get with the program." But it was not until Miss Thompson investigated the situation, that she understood the reasons for Teddy's behavior. Only then was she able to tap into the power of the true value of compassion, to change the life of this child.

This is where we are presented with opportunities.

And therein lies the rub. This is where we are presented with opportunities. Everyone can see that it's all about how "they" are behaving unskillfully. We tell ourselves that we have nothing to do with how horrible they are. They can't be changed. They will never get it. And yet, adults and children both are deeply affected and, yes, even changed by a simple act of compassion.

In my thirties, I had remarried and was raising three children in a new blended family. I was also working to create my writing and speaking career. I was stretched to the max. While I managed life peacefully most times, on one day in particular, timelines were crunched and everything that could go wrong had gone wrong. I was in a rush to get several heavy packages mailed at the post office. Just as I arrived, a woman stepped right in front of me and took my place in line. I let her know in no uncertain terms how rude she was to have been so thoughtless and inconsiderate.

With more warm compassion than I had ever experienced in my entire life, she said, "Please, please take my place. Let me help you hold something." I immediately began crying. I was so moved by her compassion for my plight in life that day that I started blubbering about how hard my day had been. She listened and nodded with that knowing, soft-hearted look. The tears poured from me like Niagara Falls! I had no idea how distressed I was until that moment.

I'd had zero compassion for myself until I received it from this most kind and generous woman. She continued to help me carry my packages until I was waited on and I will never forget her. She certainly made a difference in my life that day.

The fork in the road: when we choose compassion or judgment.

Most of us soak up compassion like a sponge when it's given to us. For me, compassion is what changes my reactions at a later time, when I'm at the fork in the road, choosing compassion or judgment.

The power of her compassion made a difference in my life for just one brief moment in time and yet the memory of it often pops in my mind when I notice people rushing about, frantic or angry at meeting life's demands. What a gift it is to let people go ahead, push in front of us if need be, and to know that maybe, in some small way, we brought some ease to their day and that this simple act was of help to them.

It's the moment that makes the difference. It's not flag-waving, march on, over-efforting that changes things. It's the moment when something done out of compassion is remembered for all time. It's fleeting. It's there, and then it's not. And the only time you remember it is when you need it.

Compassion...
frees us from attachment
to an outcome.

People like Doris Voitier don't stop to consider if the moment is right for compassion. Doris, who stepped up when needed and was honored for rebuilding her St. Bernard Parish schools in the face of Hurricane Katrina's destruction—with very little help from the bureaucracy—received the John F. Kennedy Profile in Courage Award on May 21, 2007.

During a television interview she admitted to feeling uncomfortable about being called a "hero" and receiving so much national attention for the difference she made in the aftermath of Hurricane Katrina. "I think, pre-Katrina, I was basically—as most teachers and most educators are—a rule-follower. But I quickly saw that in a crisis situation, you had to throw all that out, because nothing would get done."

Making a difference is all about diving in...

Rarely does a difference get made by rigidly adhering to a bunch of constrictive, fear-based rules. As you will see in the stories I've selected for this book, making a difference is all about diving in and simply doing the thing that's in front of us to do.

The gift in compassion is that it frees us from attachment to an outcome. When we are free, we are already making a difference by what we then model and are compelled to do for others.

To access the power of compassion, we access and embrace humanness, both our own and that of others. I know you've heard the saying, "Walk a mile in my shoes..." Well, the second you put yourself in someone else's shoes, you begin to access the heart of the matter, and therein lies innate compassion.

If you want to be blessed with all good things in life,
learn to silently bless everyone with all good things in life.
Deepak Chopra

Compassion—

For most people, the problem with being compassionate is that we fear if we offer it, we'll somehow be condoning and encouraging hurtful behavior. Yet, in a story like Teddy's, we can see right away how a life can be changed for the better, with changes lasting the span of a lifetime.

The real power of compassion is choosing it in the midst of difficult situations involving behaviors that we find upsetting and entirely off-putting. How can one be expected to be compassionate in the midst of fear?

The Universal Language of Mankind

How indeed? And yet this is what this story is all about. While it is fictional, it is most possible. From the letters I've received since the *Make A Difference* movie first appeared, I know that examples of profound compassion happen all the time, with people like you and me. If you've received this book as a gift, it's probably because you are making a difference in people's lives all the time. Have you stopped to think about the wonderful changes you're initiating?

Wouldn't it be nice if it happened even more often? That's why I'm writing. Because it is you and I, the people who read books like this, who need to reach for the power of compassion even more than we already do.

We already get it. Yet to have more people making a difference, we must keep doing it.

When others around us, children or adults, behave unskillfully or inappropriately, with actions that are intended to affront or cause harm, they need our understanding and compassion.

This is the fork in the road, where we can choose compassion... or judgment. It's important to understand that compassion does not mean that you condone hurtful or unskilled behavior. It's reaching into yourself to relate to people with a heartfelt energy of compassion that they can hear and assimilate.

If you judge people, you have no time to love them.
Mother Teresa

Every time I choose compassion, I am deeply astounded, not only at the power of this force, but that it really works to shift and change a situation.

We often miss an important point. As you go to that compassionate place within yourself to look at the person who is doing something upsetting, you are not only giving compassion, but you are also receiving what you've just given. You cannot launch a negative attitude or a judgment at someone and still feel peaceful and good about yourself. In those moments, it's impossible to feel lovable or safe.

There has been a significant amount of research about compassion, in the areas of human development and behavior.

Psychologists have demonstrated that a compassionate response to difficult people and situations yields a positive reaction 70% of the time. Whereas, responding with resentment or anger produces a negative reaction 100% of the time!

So which odds would you choose?

Compassion: Positive Result 70% of the Time
Resentment: Failure Result 100% of the Time

As I've illustrated in my book, *Attitude Alignment: The Art of Getting What You Want*, if you want the problematic situations in your life to dissipate and improve, start "throwing compassion" at the person or at the problematic behavior. I know it sounds too simple, but I invite you to try it. The next time you are upset, throw compassion at the problem and see how the situation changes before your very eyes.

This story and this little book are a small but powerful reminder of what the highest and best part of you already knows: that compassion makes us protective rather than controlling. The difference is crucial in creating long-term, life-enhancing results.

To get what you want, you must give away what you want.

Give It Away

If you want love, give it away.
If you want respect, give it away.
If you want honesty, give it away.
If you want cooperation, give it away.
If you want compassion, give it away.
If you want control, give it away!
It's really very simple when you think about it.

Mary Robinson Reynolds

Make A Difference with...

Connection

Within every one of us is a still small voice. It's a spiritual connection that cannot be seen or touched. Yet we have a way to verify invisible things by utilizing a faculty more powerful and reliable than the five senses of consciousness. We are touched by each other's stories. When we are touched, we access compassion. Compassion is our truest nature and our purest connection to spirit.

This connection never causes harm to one's self or to others.

Very simply put, spiritual connection is a sense of something greater than the self. It can be God, nature, the cosmos, a social cause, or the sea of humanity. A psychological sense of spirituality is a feeling of union and transcendence, motivated by compassion, awe, peace or joy. This remarkable connection is related in a story my husband shared with me, about his first conscious experience with the spirit of compassion in the work environment.

"A disgruntled employee had set our building on fire, and it burned hot enough to melt the computers and phones on everyone's desk in my accounting department at the small trucking company where I was controller. Within eight hours, we had phones and dispatch computers back up and running in the shop building, but the next three months were chaotic as everything in the fire-damaged area was torn down and rebuilt in record time.

"The owner of the company, an achievement-driven former truck driver demanded excellence from everyone—and was sure to let you know it if you fell short on anything. I was stressed beyond imagination, having worked seven days a week for three months, managing the computer systems' reconstruction crisis and the rebuilding. The owner was even more stressed, feeling his life's work threatened.

"Shortly before we moved back into the new building, he called me upstairs to his office. As I saw the outburst coming—it was a regular occurrence—I tensed my whole body and clenched my jaw, not to fight back, but to withstand the verbal assault. He met me at the door, red-faced, and threatened to hurl me back down the stairs. Throwing a packet of receipts in my face, he bellowed that I had failed to pay his American Express bill that month.

stressed beyond imagination.

"In the instant that he threw the bills at me, it was as if time had slowed down. I raised my arm and grabbed them out of the air before they hit me. The owner continued his verbal assault, inches from my face, but I didn't hear it. I realized immediately that I had reverted to the state of 'suspended animation' that I had used as a child, in self-defense against my father during his frequent verbal attacks.

"I had done therapy work on my relationship with my father and had come to love him, knowing that he was terribly stressed, abused and pressured by his own father. In that moment, I saw my boss in the same loving light. I almost smiled, but suppressed it, knowing that he would misinterpret it as smugness or defiance.

"Would I call it compassion? I hadn't thought of it that way at the time, but that is what it was. Compassion for my boss, for my father, and for myself. I was consciously aware that I felt something bigger than myself, a spiritual connection to all humanity. In this state of heightened awareness, it was easy—in fact, effortless—not to internalize the shame he was heaping on me. I instantly knew that missing the payment was both understandable and trivial in the circumstances; and I knew that both he and I were stretched beyond our limits.

"Then the most amazing thing happened. Instead of ending his ranting with the usual epithets and degrading remarks about my lack of performance, he started stuttering and sputtering. He seemed unable to continue with his tirade. I think he saw in my eyes the compassion I felt for him in that moment, and he was completely disarmed. He mumbled a dismissal, and I went down the stairs with a new view of the scene before me. I had a sense that it would not be long before I was working somewhere else. I had compassion as well for the many employees I would be leaving behind in this oppressive environment.

"We never talked about that incident after that, but I felt a shift in our relationship. He was still a tough boss, but he stopped intervening directly with my staff (something I'd objected to in the past) but came to me instead. While he was no less tolerant of errors than before, he seldom raised his voice against me.

"Within a few months, we mutually agreed to part company. I had been wanting out of accounting for many years, but felt stuck there. Within a short time, I was in a different job doing what I truly loved, managing customer service and systems design at a computer software company, working for a group of creative, inspired professionals.

"There's an old saying that we don't get to move on to the next levels in life until we have total peace with our current situation."

Compassion is not about complacency as you take action. We are all Angels for each other so we can reconcile what we came here to be.

Make A Difference with...

*F*amilies and friends are all about living, loving and compassion, in the face of all that we may find difficult to embrace. What a difference it makes to ease a loved one's transition! And yet we, ourselves, receive so much from the opportunity—the experience—put before us.

I'd like to introduce you to Michelle Campos. She owns a small catering business and has lived in Discovery Bay, California, for sixteen years. Michelle and her husband, parents of three and grandparents of two, have owned their own erosion control business for the last seven years. I want to share Michelle's story with you, because I feel, in its message, a deep sense of importance to us all—how compassion "gives back" in ways that are expansive and unending:

"My dearest long-time friend of 23 years, Suzanne, just passed away three days ago. My heart is sad; however, she is now soaring with the angels in a perfectly healthy body and I feel her everywhere.

"Sue was diagnosed ten months ago with a rare form of ovarian cancer which has no known cure. After undergoing several bouts of chemo, she decided to try the naturopathic approach. Her dedication and her fight to be a cancer survivor inspired me daily. About two months ago she had to sell her condo, give away almost all of her treasured possessions and move in with her son and daughter-in-law. They have a wonderfully warm home and they created a beautiful room for her, with windows to look out of, waterfalls and flowers to gaze at. It was a peaceful place.

Transitions

My body's a mess but my spirit is soaring!

"She graciously surrendered to the 'process' as she'd called it. Many times people would ask, 'How are you doing?' and she'd say, 'Well, my body is really a mess but my spirit is soaring!'

"Sue knew her time was short and soon Hospice was called, so she could be comfortable in her last days. As her friend, I treasured the hours spent with her, talking and sharing our memories over the years. This last week was especially precious, with her sharing my love and gratefulness for having her in my life. I'd lie on the bed with her for hours, reassuring her it was okay to let go.

"She has raised two wonderful sons who lavished her with love and tenderness until the very end. My memory of her final day with us was of her sons placing orchids around her pillow, rubbing her feet and hands while playing beautiful music for her, telling her over and over how much they loved her.

"She was covered with a beautiful purple pareo and looked like an angel ready for the next journey of her life. The biggest blessing was that her son and daughter-in-law were blessed with a baby just two weeks before her passing. They'd been trying to adopt for over a year and little Aayden entered their lives just in time! Sue got to hold him and be blessed by his sweet presence.

"I realize how fortunate I was to be with Sue, to talk to her, even though she couldn't respond with words...she knew my voice and my touch. It felt complete and I knew I could let her go.

"I will miss her every day, I will miss her laughter, her endless energy and the hundreds of phone calls. I will miss dancing with her and just taking long walks. She has left a lasting imprint on my heart. Soar my beautiful friend and someday we will be together again!"

You give but little when you give of your possessions.
It is when you give of yourself that you truly give.

Kahlil Gibran

Make A Difference with...

Grandchildren

$\mathcal{W}$hen I told my Texan friend, Kate Nowak, a mother of three, grandmother of eight and great-grandmother of one, about writing this book, she immediately recalled a touching story about how her granddaughter had made a difference in her life. Kate is the creator of the online movie *May You Be Blessed* which can also be seen at our MakeADifference.com website.

"When my granddaughter, Heather, was a little girl, it was my delight to be able to watch over her during the day while her parents worked. Though usually a happy toddler, on one particular day, Heather awakened from her nap in a cranky mood, and from her perspective nothing seemed to be going right.

Her temper erupted in all its tiny fury...

"Aggravated because she couldn't get a toy to work as she wanted, her temper finally erupted in all its tiny fury and in the midst of the resulting

tantrum, she knocked over a small vase I kept on a nearby table, spilling water and scattering the few flowers it contained across the floor.

"'Don't act that way, Sweetheart,' I scolded as I cleaned up the mess made by the spill. 'You hurt Granny's feelings when you treat my things that way.'

"A few minutes later, having left Heather to play in her toy room while I unloaded the dishwasher, I was surprised when she came to me and tugged on my shirt for attention. 'I'm so sorry, Granny,' she said, her bottom lip quivering, her big brown eyes pooled with tears, one spilling over to run down her cheek. 'I wouldn't hurt you for anything.'

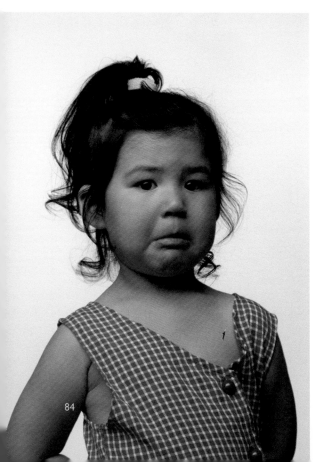

"I reached down and scooped her little body into my arms and held her tight as the last remnants of her fragile composure vanished and she broke into sobs, her little face wet with tears as she burrowed her head against my neck.

"Tears sprang into my own eyes and for several minutes we stood there in my kitchen, holding on to each other for dear life, my heart as touched by her pain as hers had been touched by her perception of mine.

"Until that day, I had always thought that as a responsible parent and grandparent, compassion and kindness were traits I needed to instill in the children placed within my care.

Children come with kindness and compassion built right in.

"Heather taught me, however, that children come with kindness and compassion built right in. Our job is not to instill it, but to nurture it and watch as it grows and blossoms."

In one hundred years, it won't matter what house you lived in,
what car you drove, or even what your clothes looked like.
What will matter is that you made a difference in the life of a child.

Dr. Forest E. Witcraft

Make a Difference with...
Courage

This next story is a most exquisite account of how one woman's compassion actually helped create a family. I am deeply struck by the unbridled power of this nurse's story, and not only because my very own firstborn child was lost to us at birth. I know the power of holding your baby in your arms to say hello and good–bye. But this story is also an illustration of great courage. She did what was right, and it made a profound difference in the lives of these parents and their ability to go forward into a beautiful future. Here is Dolly Adriatico's story:

She did what was right and it made a profound difference...

"Many years ago as a young nurse, I worked on an OB-GYN unit in a hospital. I loved being around mothers–to–be and their new babies. One woman I cared for had already lost four babies who were born prematurely, and she was in the process of losing her fifth. It was an incredibly sad event for everyone on the unit, and I couldn't think of a way to console her.

"As she cried to me about her loss, she felt it was especially tragic, since this particular baby was the one she had carried the longest. The other four were lost early on in the pregnancy, but she had a special bond with this fifth baby, for she could feel him kick and move inside her. She said she wished she could just hold him for a little while, and touch him, as it would make the whole experience more real for her.

She wished she could hold him for just a little while...

"'Do you want to hold your baby?' I blurted out, knowing that in those days, this was an unheard-of event on our unit.

"My brain kicked into high gear, trying to figure out how I could possibly arrange this very controversial (at the time) meeting of new mother and deceased child without getting fired. Both the woman and her husband looked at me with pleading eyes and asked, 'Can we hold our baby, please? It would mean so much to us.' Now, there was no stopping me. I had to make someone in authority listen to me and find a way to get this new baby to its parents.

"After speaking with the parents a few more minutes, I made the decision to pursue this course for them, and I went to speak to my supervisor.

"'What! They want to hold their baby? Haven't they been through enough?' my supervisor said.

"I convinced her to go and talk to the parents, and also convinced a social worker to sit in on the event for support. Within a half hour, the newly deceased baby was wheeled to the room where his parents waited. It was one of the saddest and happiest moments I have ever witnessed.

"Sad, because the baby had died, of course, but happy, because he was so perfect. A beautiful cap of dark wavy hair covered his tiny little scalp, ten fingers and ten toes and luscious long eyelashes. The baby looked as if he were sleeping peacefully while his parents wept silently over his loss. After a short time, the parents were ready to relinquish the baby and he was returned to the morgue.

"I spoke with them about the experience of holding the baby, and the mother said something I could almost understand at the time—and now that I have children of my own, I completely understand what she meant.

"She said that they both knew the baby had died, and that they'd have plenty of time to see him and hold him at the funeral, but that they wanted to spend time with him before the funeral setting.

"At least for one moment, they could pretend he was alive and just sleeping, and that was something they had never experienced with their other losses. She said she just wanted to feel what it's like to be a mother, even if it's only for a few moments. Both she and her husband thanked me profusely and we parted ways at the end of the shift.

"When I went to work the next day I was really hurt to learn that she'd left the hospital without so much as a thank you to me. I was young and inexperienced, but I guess I'd have been happy with a 'thanks' written on a scrap of paper towel. Here I was, thinking the whole night of the event that I'd actually made a difference to someone and this was what nursing was all about.

"To my delight and surprise, three years later, a letter from this mother arrived on the unit for me. She thanked me again for my kindness that day, and she was happy to report to me that she and her husband had adopted three siblings and all were doing well.

"She also said that she kept that feeling of being a mother and held it in her heart all this time, but that the loss was just a dull ache now, as she had become a real mother to three children—and she *feels* like a mother every day now.

"Did I make a difference to her? I like to think so. But she made a difference for me too."

I don't need to tell you how powerful this story is on so many different levels. However the point I want to make here is that so often we think our actions have not made a significant difference—and that can be disheartening.

What's important here is to take heart in those moments.   Remembering always that you receive the instant you give and, in that, you can trust you've made a difference in someone's life, because you felt it in your own.

You can trust you've made a difference in someone's life, because you felt it in your own.

Make A Difference with...
Education

"I was touched by your movie.
We all know that good teachers make a positive difference each day.
Sometimes we just need to be reminded."

Doris Voitier, Superintendent, St. Bernard Parish Schools
and recipient of the *JFK Profile in Courage Award*

Whatever we focus on—put our attention on—expands.

What is important to focus upon is not what's wrong with our schools today, but all the good that truly, truly, is happening there. As we approach problematic areas in education, we can do it with an attitude of gratitude and with the understanding we can make a difference. From administration all the way down to individual children who need to be brought into our fold, we will find the most creative, simple and satisfying ways to accomplish this...with compassion.

Education

Deb Booth, an almost–49–year old, has in her professional life worn lots of hats—actress, hairdresser, radio announcer, legal secretary, photographer, librarian and writer. She's a proud mom to two successful kids. Deb's been married to the same man for almost 26 years, and she feels lucky to live in a 137-year-old farmhouse in a small town nestled in the foothills of the Blue Ridge mountains in Virginia. Here is her story, about how her daughter is making a difference in education, a difference that affects three generations:

"I believe that what you give out is what you get back—so give Joy. My daughter, Bree, began her first year of teaching this year, after securing a Master's in Elementary Education at the University of Virginia. She accepted a position in the Rosa Parks Elementary School in Dale City, Virginia, teaching a great class of third graders.

"We've all heard about how the next generation is uncaring, but what happened this week completely dispelled that erroneous notion for me.

"Bree has found time to be able to add extras to her curriculum—extras that highlight her caring, empathetic nature. After the first 100 days of class, she asked her students to write "100 Pieces of Praise," about something for which they were grateful—something very definitely not material in nature.

"One student was grateful that his friend's broken arm had healed. One was grateful for a friend who made her laugh—it gave her butterflies, she said. The list of the simple, and not-so-simple things for which these young folks were grateful was inspiring, funny and poignant.

"But what truly brought me joy, and hope—was one of Bree's lessons on compassion. My mother is a lung transplant patient, in stage 4 kidney failure and on dialysis three times a week. She's tired and uncomfortable most of the time, while feeling pretty danged discouraged.

95

"Bree mentioned this to the children and asked what they would say if they wanted to cheer someone up—something other than 'Hey, I hope you feel better.'

"She provided them with some left-over remnants of construction paper, some glue and glitter, markers, pens and tissue paper and asked them to create Compassion Notes to send to her grandmother.

"The notes were colorful, ranging from the simple to the profound. My eyes teared up several times as I read them, even as I laughed out loud at the expressions, thoughts and spelling used.

What made it especially poignant was what happened after the notes were written.

"The story would have been fine, but what made it especially poignant for me, was what happened after the notes were written.

"One of the students, Cam, wrote this note: 'Hi, whoever you are. I will train a monkey to make you happy. It can juggle to make you laugh.'

"He approached Bree one day and asked if she'd delivered the compassion notes to her grandmother yet. Bree said no, she hadn't, but would be seeing her grandma that weekend.

"Cam told Bree that he actually had a stuffed monkey, and that he'd like her grandmother to have it, if Bree thought she would like it.

"Bree, sensing that perhaps the monkey had significant emotional value to Cam, tried to dissuade him, but he persisted. He was ready to give it up, he didn't play with it (much) any more and if it would make Bree's grandmother happy, then he wanted to give it to her. Maybe it would make her feel better.

"He brought it in and a fine, well–loved monkey it was, too. Bree laid it gently atop the other notes in the gaily decorated gift bag and brought it to my mother.

A fine, well-loved monkey it was, too.

"My mother smiled as she lifted the monkey from the colored tissue paper in the bag, saying this was obviously someone's beloved toy.

"Was Bree sure that she was meant to have it? Bree nodded—she was sure. Mom read the notes that were in the bag and she laughed, and she cried, she grinned, and she giggled...and she cried some more.

"She ended the reading by asking Bree to please pass back to Cam her promise that if he ever—ever—wanted his monkey back, she would send it posthaste.

She found a way to include lessons on compassion, praise and empathy.

"Can I just tell you how happy I am that Bree has found a way to include lessons on compassion, praise and empathy along with the standard curriculum of reading, 'riting and 'rithmatic?

"Can I tell you how much hope it gave me, to realize that these young people had been encouraged to look beyond themselves to think of others and to have been given the opportunity to try to alleviate someone else's pain—someone they didn't know?

"I tried to explain to Bree why I was crying, as I was telling her about reading those notes. I tried to express my wonder at how she has touched the future by opening these children's minds and hearts, and I hope she understood.

They'll pass on what they've learned about the human heart.

"There is hope for the future. It's embodied by the valiant struggle to live, made by a woman weakened by disease, feeling worn and ill. It is embodied by a young woman teaching her first year of school, adding 'extra' lessons to the standard required fare.

"It's embodied by a class of third graders, who laugh and nudge each other over 'potty humor,' who cry when they miss the bus, but who spent time, and effort trying to cheer up someone they'd never even met.

"With any luck at all—with any grace this Universe can provide—these kids will be able to pass what they have learned about the human heart on to their friends, and their own children...and so on, and so on, and so on.

"Ad infinitum."

Make A Difference with ...
Purpose

Our gifts and our talents are our business in life; they are our purpose. It is in the reaching out in purpose that we receive the joy of passion. Without purpose, passion, and a sense that we are making a difference, what meaning does our life really have, and why should we strive to do our best work? As I heard author Brian Tracy once say: "You are the CEO of your own service organization."

How often do we think of compassion as it relates to the business of sales?

I find it interesting that so many people minimize the importance of the job of a salesperson, without recognizing that this is truly a business of service. We are all in the business of sales. When you want your spouse to take you out on a date to see a movie, you are immediately in the business of sales. Our children practice sales techniques every single time they try to sell us on the advantages of a new toy.

What we often fail to realize is that the business of sales is actually a form of education. The salesperson's original intention is to teach people about products that can and do have the potential to make a difference in their lives simply by the ease and comfort they bring.

The gift is always in the giving—meaning that we receive as we give. This heartwarming story of one woman's experience in direct sales explains this contrarian concept.

The gift is always in the giving— meaning that we receive as we give.

Kathleen Pulsipher, her sister, and two brothers were raised in Utah by loving parents. She found her one true love in 1975, at the age of 24, and together they nurtured thirteen foster children and raised four beautiful adopted children.

Kathleen became a Mary Kay skin care consultant in 1993, a job which has been a blessing to her in so many ways, from overcoming shyness, to meeting the most amazing people during her fourteen years as a consultant.

Her story is most inspiring to people of all industries and professions, those who are encouraged to make a difference because of that strong, insistent pull inside them. Here is her beautiful story:

"I had been a Mary Kay consultant for about three years when I met a woman who was very excited to be treated to a complimentary pampering session. I remember that the day was bright and sunshiny. I pulled up to her home, which looked nice on the outside, and I rang the doorbell. She opened the door and invited me in. In fact, she was so excited to have me come, but to my surprise, there was no furniture in her home, except for a small kitchen table with two chairs.

"The woman and I sat and chatted for a moment and then I set up my products for her makeup session. She couldn't have been more excited to get started. At the end of our time, I asked the usual question, 'What could I help you with today?'

"She wanted every product that she had tried that morning. Yet in the back of my mind, all I could think about was the fact that she had no furniture. So it came as no surprise when she told me that she could not pay me today, but that she had a welfare check coming in the next day or two. Could I please hold her order until then, and at that time, she'd like it all. I wrote the entire order down for her, knowing that cosmetics were not what she needed, but some furniture instead.

"I packed up my products and supplies and was ready to leave. My heart felt heavy. I knew it was not right to take her money, so I was not going to have a new customer or sale. She walked out to my car, helping me to carry my cases. When we said goodbye, she suddenly gave me a big hug, one I knew was sincere. Tears began to trickle down her face as she told me, 'I am so pretty, I am so pretty—thank you for sharing your time with me. I will have money in a few days.'

I will always carry this
paycheck of the heart' with me.

"I hugged her back with a heart that felt so free and loving. I knew at that moment that I had been given the biggest paycheck I could ever receive. No, I never saw or heard from her again, but I knew that two lives had been touched that day. I have been a Mary Kay consultant now for fourteen years and will always carry this 'paycheck of the heart' with me. Thank you for allowing me to share this precious moment with you today.

"Is there a direct correlation between true compassion and the prosperity of a business? Most definitely, yes! Mary Kay Ash, the founder of Mary Kay, has always taught us that people have an invisible sign around their neck that says, 'Make me feel important.' She is absolutely right. People want to feel that they matter. When customers feel good about themselves they are receptive to what you would like to share with them. You need to take the dollar signs out of your eyes and be truly sincere in helping and making a person feel good, first and foremost. The sale in most cases will follow but, again, getting customers to feel great about themselves is the ultimate sale that we can make with a person.

"Always remember that whatever you give to people, you will get returned tenfold."

Make A Difference with ...
Humanity

Over a decade ago, I heard a memorable quote from Maya Angelou, where she said, "You may not remember what people say or do, but you'll never forget how they made you feel."

Any community, anywhere in the world, is made up of ordinary people doing extraordinary things.

We often think that giving back to our community requires a great effort or huge time commitment. It must be labor-intensive in order to count—or so we think. Not so! How we connect with our communities is how we heal humanity. It's really all about what happens with one person, one interaction at a time.

Here is a story from a young woman by the name of Ellen Sperry who writes about the meaning of making a difference, then having it returned in amazing proportions. Ellen is a 43-year-old single mother of a perfect fourteen-year-old daughter. Her careers have been varied: graphic artist, personal assistant, teacher's assistant, potter, and Mom.

She feels that, "it's a life of nothing extraordinary, but many extraordinary moments, that I interpret as the divine hand at work." Here is her story for humanity:

*I was feeling a lack of faith
with some situations in my life.*

"I go to the beach each morning after I drop my child at school, to meditate, to connect with spirit and to simply start my day. On one particular morning, I was feeling a lack of faith with some situations in my life. I journaled and meditated, and I still wasn't quite getting it. I often speak to spirit as an intimate companion.

"One morning, I asked to be shown what it is I am supposed to do, asked to let me know I have been heard, and stated my vow to be an instrument for peace, to communicate always from an intention of love.

I asked to be shown what it is I am supposed to do.

"As I was leaving the beach, a very old man was sitting on the beach at the pavilion. He started to talk to me, but his speech was slurred and he was hard to hear clearly. At first, because my mind was so occupied with my own problems, I almost just gave him a wave, with a hurried, 'Have a good day,' as I rushed to get on with my own life. Instead I just sat down with him. And we talked.

"I was able to understand him clearly, even though he had very few teeth and was a bit senile. We talked for half an hour. He had a collection of shields attached to his belt, as if he'd once been a police officer. I asked him about them. He took every one off and showed me. They were fake—from a 'five and dime' type of store—but to him they were real. He said his name was Pat and he lived four blocks away. He asked me if I needed a home and I told him no because I already had one.

"He described how he had survived three types of cancer and the doctors told him he was going to die. He told me of all his hospital visits. How they were cleaning the beach nicely today, how Timmy the cop was going to give him another badge. How he doesn't come here in the rain or cold. I just listened and listened and asked him questions.

"There were two gentlemen eating breakfast sandwiches at the pavilion, they kept looking over to me, with perplexed looks on their faces as I was talking to this senile, dirty, old crazy man—with his cardigan sweater tucked into his pants and with a belt full of false badges—and I could not have been happier.

I slowed down, I did what was in front of me to do...
And what a gift I did receive!

"Toward the end of our conversation, tears came to my eyes, for I once again knew that my connection to that which breathes me was real, that all of humanity and the Infinite was living in this old man sitting on a bench in a pavilion—and he was my gift today. A place I walk by every morning of my life and yet I have never seen him before. I slowed down, I did what was in front of me to do, which was to acknowledge another human being's desire to connect with me, without my prejudice getting in the way. And what a gift I did receive on that day. How blessed I truly am. How Pat did give me a home today, my home with all that is, one I had forgotten for a moment."

*C*ompassion is sometimes
the fatal capacity for feeling
what it is like to live inside
somebody else's skin.

It is the knowledge that
there can never really be
any peace and joy for
me until there is peace
and joy finally for you too.

Frederick Buechner

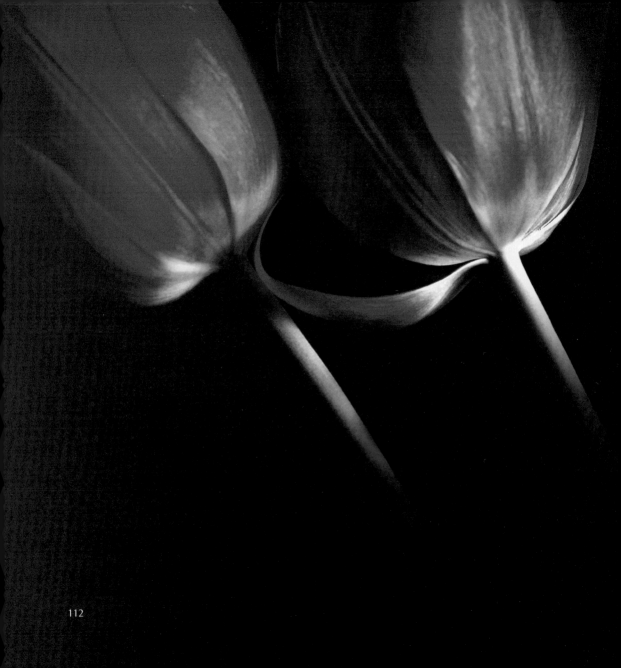

An Instrument of Peace...

*I*t is as important to be a good recipient of the gift of compassion as it is to be the giver. Or are they really any different?

On those occasions when I feel inwardly directed to hand money to a person who is asking for money at freeway exits or grocery store parking lots, I have had some of the most profound, amazing and mystical experiences of my life.

I'll never forget the first time it happened. I was coming up an off-ramp and I saw, on the left side of my vehicle, a father standing with his teen-age son.   It was probably because of the boy that I felt an urgent need to reach quickly into my pocket book and pull out any cash I could find. Two twenties landed in my fingers and I rolled down my window to reach out and hand it to the father.

As he reached out and gently took the money from my hand, he looked directly and deeply in my eyes and as he touched my soul he said, "God bless you." In that instant, I immediately felt a deep connection. The light changed and I forced myself to drive. I was so overwhelmed with a world of feelings in that moment. I felt it all. The world of suffering and pain. The world of ecstasy and wonder. The world of amazing light and love enveloped me and all I could do was weep and weep and weep some more, deeply, from my soul.

I pulled off the side of the road, because I couldn't even drive. I was so overcome by what had just happened.

It matters not to me what people who ask for money actually do with the money. It's all about what happens as we look into each other's eyes and souls. It is something I can, in fact, give that has the potential to make a lasting difference. Miss Thompson didn't attach the level of her giving to what Teddy would or wouldn't do with it. She simply thought about Teddy compassionately because it was what was needed.

There is a presence and a power that breathes within every single one of us.

There is a presence and a power that breathes within every single one of us. No matter what we call it, it's inside each and every one of us. Yet compassion calls it forth in ways that are beyond our human understanding. How compassion works is a mystery as deep as spirit itself. With compassion, there is a whole range of positive possibilities.

Research about the brain reveals that compassionate thoughts literally light up the frontal lobe of a person's brain. (The frontal lobe is where the mind can access solutions.) When we are resentful or angry, there is no light in that part of the brain, and so we shut down and fail to function well. As soon as we deliberately think compassionate thoughts, this part of the brain lights up, and we can literally go from "impossible" to "possible" in an instant.

Whether you are devoutly religious or deeply spiritual, an atheist, an agnostic or a skeptic, when you simply decide to think compassionate thoughts, the power of the feeling that is ignited is palpable. The connection is instantly available and deeply real.

Compassion is, after all, a deep awareness of the suffering of another, coupled with the wish to relieve it.

It is truly wanting others to be free from suffering. And when we offer this, we have made a difference.

The compassion within is what makes the difference.

Make me an instrument of your peace and when I have gone, then I have done what I came here to do.

Compassionately,

Mary Robinson Reynolds

Acknowledgments

In acknowledgment of my editor and book designer, Heather Kibbey of Northwest Publishers Consortium, Lake Oswego, OR, (npcbooks.com)—woman extraordinaire, as I call her—who thrilled me every day with her creative inspiration and genius for this book. I think you'll agree with me, that what she has done with this book is amazing, profound and has heartfelt beauty. One of the most enjoyable aspects for me as a writer is when I begin to see my words come to life in the book formatting process. Every day with Heather's incoming page designs is like opening present after present. My gift-receiving quotient has been abundantly filled for this year!

I'd like to give a heartfelt thanks to my sister, Markreta Brandt for her "last look" editing expertise in each and every book I've written since my first book, *You Are A Success!*—almost twenty years ago.

It's important to me to acknowledge and introduce you to my amazing MasterMind partners, Craig Reynolds, Judy Pearson and Kate Nowak, for without them life would be difficult, not to mention bland.

First, my husband Craig. I must say he signed on for quite an adventure when he married me. Not only was I a mother of a young son, I was very ill at the time. I'd overextended myself in an effort to create a career as a professional speaker and author. Previous marriages brought their own stresses into this "let's make a difference" journey. Through a spiritual goal achieving process—known as MasterMinding—we've been able to build a rich life and marriage filled with enjoyment of each other and our truly wonderful children.

When two or more people coordinate in a spirit of harmony and work toward a definite objective or purpose, they place themselves in position, through this alliance, to absorb power directly from the great storehouse of Infinite Intelligence.

Napoleon Hill, author of *Think & Grow Rich.*

Judy Pearson, author of *Say "Yes!" to Life*—has been my MasterMind partner for over a decade. She was there for me in the process of seeking the solutions I needed for every single challenging situation I was learning to come up over. In the early years, every week we MasterMinded, I asked and kept my focus, intention and feeling of receiving it upon the goal. Every week, I did not entirely believe that what I would ask for was possible, but Judy always did! Because of her willingness to simply see for me the goals that are bigger than anything I could possibly do by myself, together we move mountains for all good.

Kate Nowak saw my first flash online movie, *You Are The Light Movie*, and when she learned I wrote about MasterMinding, she said to herself, "I wish I could MasterMind with Mary." Several months later she came out with a beautiful movie, *May You Be Blessed* and one day, out of the blue, I felt it was important to call her and ask her if she wanted to be MasterMind partners. Talk about a quick result to a heartfelt desire! We've had nothing but creative fun with achieving our goals together since!

Finally, I'd like to acknowledge the hundreds of people who sent me their stories about the power of compassion and specifically the ones whose stories defined the direction this book wanted to take: the story of *Connection*, Craig Reynolds; *Transition*, Michelle Campos; *Grandchildren*, Kate Nowak; *Courage*, Dolly Adriatico; *Education*, Deb Booth; *Purpose*, Kathleen Pulsipher; and *Humanity*, Ellen Sperry.

There is no better way to be *making a difference* in the places you work or in the lives of those around you than to learn how you can join with others—in the spirit of harmony—to MasterMind your way through problematic situations and create new solutions to the opportunities in front of you. I don't know of anyone who has become super successful who has not employed the principle of MasterMinding in some form.

When several people focus on your goals, your dreams and your opportunities, it's like putting lightning in a bottle. It is this spiritual aspect that Napoleon Hill wrote about extensively. He said that if we are in tune with the MasterMind—that is, whatever term you use for the all-powerful creative life force—we have significantly more positive energy available to us, a power that can be focused on our success.

May we all be instruments of Peace,   *Mary Robinson Reynolds*

Educational Psychology, Counseling & Development

Mary Robinson Reynolds, an educational psychologist, master trainer, is the author of five books: *Make A Difference...with the Power of Compassion, Attitude Alignment: The Art of Getting What You Want!, No Labels No Limits, You Are A Success!, MasterMinding for a Rich Life, MasterMinding 101®* online course and *Stay Married* online course.

As a professional speaker, Mary's dynamic presentation range covers the spectrum from subtle, spiritual and endearing to outrageously, side-splittingly funny, to hammer-the-point intensity. She is also a wise and somewhat bawdy soul, masterful at helping others trust that what they desire is valid.

As an author, she writes as she speaks, with vocabulary that's familiar and funny. Her advice is direct, not airy-fairy encouragement, to get people going with the changes they know they need to make. She opens your 'soul' with gentle, probing questions like, "So how do you really prefer it to be?" and "Why do you think you can't have it?"

There is nothing more important to Mary than her husband, children and extended family and friends. She feels she lives an amazingly rich life, having put her connection to spirit first, her family second and purpose and passion for world healing and peace third. Her husband, Craig, was able to join her in the production of online flash movies and publishing business in 2004. She feels her greatest of all achievements is her blended family with her husband's two daughters and her son.

Life should NOT be a journey to the grave with the intention of arriving safely in an attractive and well-preserved body, but rather to skid in sideways, chocolate in one hand, wine in the other, body thoroughly used up, totally worn out and screaming, "Woo-Hoo what a ride!"

Mavis Leyrer of Seattle, age 83

Elizabeth Silance Ballard's short stories and articles have appeared in many magazines since 1974 including *Our State, The Australian Women's Weekly, Home Life, Mature Living, Mature Years, The Organist, The Church Musician, The Organ Portfolio, The Music Leader, The Gospel Choir, The Lutheran Woman, The Lutheran Scope, The Mennonite, Quaker Life* and many others. Several anthologies have included her work, such as *A Second Helping of Chicken Soup for the Soul* (credit was omitted in the 1st printing but corrected in the 2nd printing), *Stories for a Woman's Heart, More Stories for a Woman's Heart, Stories for a Teacher's Heart, Stories for a Teen's Heart, School Bells and Ink Wells, Kisses of Sunshine,* and others. Her work has also been included in other publications such as *Divergent Views on the Control of Schools: An Iowa Dialogue, Discipline for Life* and others.

Her short story, "Three Letters from Teddy," first appeared in 1974 and has been almost continuously in print every year since that time in various publications. Marian Wright Edelman selected it to appear in her *1994 Annual Report* of the National Children's Defense Fund. Congressman Dan Burton, Indiana, requested permission to have the story reprinted and distributed to every educator in his district. It has also been selected for the course packs of the schools of education in several universities including the University of South Florida, University of North Carolina–Greensboro, University of Northern Iowa and others.

Elizabeth is a retired social worker, a church organist, a pianist, and is the mother of two and grandmother of three. She has traveled extensively in the U.S. and abroad and enjoys reading, writing, needlework and line dancing. She is active in her church and the Order of the Eastern Star.

Her recent book, *Three Letters from Teddy...and Other Stories,*
is available at: www.MakeADifference.com

Author of "Three Letters From Teddy" – © Elizabeth Silance Ballard
Storyteller: Craig Reynolds, Heart Productions & Publishing
Background Music: *Innocence* by Brady Barnett, provided by StudioCutz.com
Cover background texture: imageafter.com
Photographers: I'd like to express my appreciation to the photographers whose images contributed to our *Make A Difference* movie and this beautiful gift book, most of whom are represented by istockphotos.com, photos.com and gettyphotos.com:

Don Bayley	Byron Kibbey	Kevin Peterson
DAJ	Tomaz Levstek	Amanda Rohde
Digital Vision	Miroslaw Andrzej Oslizlo	Wouter van Caspel
Joseph Jean Rolland Dubé	Thomas Polen	Daniel Vineyard
Oleksandr Gumerov	Stephen Pottage	Yellow Dog Productions
	Oleg Prikhodko	

I'd like to give special recognition to the following photographers:

Leah-Anne Thompson, whose photos of Teddy Stallard appear in the book and movie, actually photographed her own son as Teddy, at the corresponding ages. At the printing of this book he was a 5th grader. His mother says he has always loved to act, even as a toddler or when not in front of a camera. Her photos appear on pages 15,16, 25, 26, 29, and 36 of *Make A Difference* movie.

Roberta Osborne is a professional photographer who has a beautiful portfolio of self-photography. She is the teacher, Miss Thompson, in our flash movie. Her photos appear on pages 12, 19, 22, 31, 35, and 53 of *Make A Difference* movie.

Debbie Del Tejo was born in the Dominican Republic and grew up in New York City. She is a photographer specializing in documentary weddings, engagements, fine art of maternity, children, seniors and special events. As a mother of one son and a grandmother of four, she knows the importance of documenting all the special and wonderful moments in a child's life. Her most recent achievement was winning the Second Place in the Flowers category at the BetterPhoto contest, from over 23,500 entries (see her winning photo, *Don't Cry* on page 112). Other photos appear on pages 46, 47, 66, 67, 106, 107, and 115 of this book. To purchase prints of her photos from this book, visit: www.MakeADifference.com

TAKE THE NEXT STEPS WITH HEART PUBLISHING & PRODUCTION

Make A Difference Flash Online Movie is part of a series of inspirational movies created by Heart Productions & Publishing's Founder, Mary Robinson Reynolds.

For more inspiration from our movies please visit us at:

www.MakeADifference.com

At our website you can join our free *Make A Difference Newsletter*, and watch our inspirational movies daily, to enjoy the benefits of a peaceful, renewed mind, body and spirit.

Popular gift items are available, such as meaningful Jewelry, full color Prints of the select photography used in this book, motivational Posters, Screensavers, Downloadable Movies and DVDs, Online Courses, Interactive and Inspirational books.

You are welcome to send our free flash online movie to those you appreciate and care about:

www.MakeADifferenceMovie.com

Sit back, relax and let Mary's movies lift you up

so you can make a difference in someone's life today!

info@MakeADifference.com

1-800-639-8191

Make A Difference with the Power of Compassion
...and we will see World Peace in Our Lifetime.

What others have said about:

MAKE A DIFFERENCE: WITH THE POWER OF COMPASSION

"Thanks for the information about your gift books...I found your books to be the best gifts in life, ones that I can treasure forever."

Fernando M. Pantino, Department of Education,
Pasig City, Manila, Philippines

"You start reading this book and it touches chords all over the place. There are stories within the *Make A Difference* Gift Book that everyone can relate to, no matter who you are, what your walk of life is, there is something in the book that will touch you in a way that will ignite a desire and you want to be more compassionate in your dealings with all people."

Kate Nowak, author of *May You Be Blessed* Movie

"Your new gift book is fantastic. I was riveted—proof, it's after midnight—meant to be in bed a couple of hours ago. I love the references to us all being big kids inside—bringing it right home to the grownups—if I'm like them, then they're like me. You make it easy to 'get' how important and universally needed compassion really is, and how far reaching in its transformations. I'll be reading it again and again, and already have a list of people I want to gift the book to."

Miché Onaclea, Sumiche Jewelry

As a TurnAround Specialist and MasterMinding Maven®, Mary Robinson Reynolds founded Heart Productions and Publishing in 1990, to build on her success as an educator, coach, consultant, entrepreneur, speaker and author.

Heart Productions & Publishing creates and markets inspirational products that meet the needs of all people wanting to heal their lives in areas of relationships, time, health and money.

Since its inception, Mary's primary interest has been to lift and elevate people working on the matters of the heart. So our goal, like our name, is to heal people's minds and hearts and to renew their spirits.

If you have enjoyed this book and wish to learn more about our flash online movies and our full line of beautifully designed products and resources that really do make a difference, please visit us at:

www.MakeADifference.com

Millions of people throughout the world are being uplifted and inspired by Mary's movies. Compelling mind–body–spirit research concludes that music has the power to reduce stress, enhance cognitive functioning, and improve productivity and creativity. Music, combined with inspired messages of hope, restores faith, renews the mind and opens the way for peaceful solutions.

Mary is a woman with a big philanthropic heart. She has created a simple system to assist people and organizations who are making a difference. If you would like to use Mary's "word of mouse" movie and Gift Book in a campaign to expand the reach of your organization (exponentially) and to raise money, simply click on the Fundraising link at our website and read how we can help you help others.

For corporate gift–giving and incentive programs, please call:
800-639-8191

ATTITUDE ALIGNMENT: "A gentle art that, once learned, will change your life..."

Now it's your turn. With *Make A Difference ...with the Power of Compassion*, you have already taken a step toward a greater humanity. Don't stop here. Take the next step and learn

Attitude Alignment—The Art of Getting What You Want

Attitude Alignment doesn't require affrontive tactics or a bullying approach. It's a gentle art that, once learned, will change your life. We each have within us the seeds to a better future. When we discover The Art of Getting What We Want, we'll step out of powerlessness and move into a life of strength and resolve.

Are you faced with a problem that appears hopeless? Is another person's hostility or indifference standing between you and your goal? When adversity strikes, have you been taught to put up your dukes and fight it out? Or do you give up, accept your fate, and settle for less than what you really want? Take heart!

Discover how attitudes (your own and those of others) shape your life. In fact, science shows us that:

You can't have an attitude and keep it a secret!

To get what you want in life—more love and respect, or money, time or enjoyment—it's first necessary to:

- Recognize what messages you project, whether you mean to or not.
- Identify and rewrite negative "labels" you've accepted from others.
- Understand how you take on other people's negativity.
- Read attitudinal energy accurately without projecting.
- Learn how to align major differences and divisions among people.
- Transform negative experiences instantly.
- Increase your credibility and your *power to influence*.

"Your book was right on target! It made me think, and take a look at the relationships in my life, and now I will take action where needed in my attitude first, actions second. Thank you very much for this body of work!"
Sondra Nolan, Roads & Rights-of-Way

To learn more about this irresistible book please visit us at:
www.AttitudeAlignment.com